LAY STUDIES

LAY STUDIES

Steven Toussaint

Victoria University Press

VICTORIA UNIVERSITY PRESS
Victoria University of Wellington
PO Box 600 Wellington
vup.victoria.ac.nz

A catalogue record is available at the National Library of New Zealand

ISBN 9781776562404

Printed by Printlink, Wellington

for Eleanor

Temps, aevum, éternité

CONTENTS

THE NEW LAITY

The final poem is praise, but this is the first
    transmission, an emergency test
of audience participation in light of recent
    unforeseeable events.
In a series of yes or no questions
    we will ask you to refresh
your annual commitment . . .
    The radio rests
but your neighbourhood remains
    a moment longer ringing, property
outperforming silence, whose articulation
    and attack need practice
to appreciate, hands immersed in soil
    up to your wedding
band, to introduce to all below the things with which
    you feel. This is the seminal
trespass, in which the slow eyes of the witness
    meet the quick eyes of the reader
and for an instant the pattern is complete
    but not foreclosed.
The earth tenders her apprentice.
    Listen to her knowledge
age, the groaning of your neighbour's second garage
    going up, the speculator's
only music. Wasn't it *fraternitas*'s fruit you wanted
    cordoned off, gauging
each depression with a fingernail, forcing

every germ into the vacant
columns you'd proportioned to goad the berries
    big? Or would you dig
a single plot, and pour them in, because
    you find it beautiful
that creatures couple up to live? The plant betrays
    no atom of a self save
friable tilth, analogies for wealth you cannot speak so
    secrete away, now a skill
you know by the way the patterns lace and purl who blew
    the glass you see them through.

ACTS

To begin again, the deepest palace must explode
unnoticed. A slow release
will always leave the one who authored you afraid.
That was legion talking from my head,
the beast. I would burn
the pages, all evidence my sentence stayed
to cheat my way inside a shadow of the rock.

POUND

Unobvious site of anchorage, as Erebus was
an isthmus zoned only for sacrifice.
I envy Odysseus
that inundated shelf he slaughtered
the lambs on, if nothing else a place
to have knelt down, awaiting the shadow
instructors, an apparition anywhere
the ritual touched, their footprints
brimming with blood.

But the flensing is never finished
when the offering outlives its mystery
recipient. Tiresias starves, doubly
damned, whispering
                              SERVIAM

ST. FRANCIS

That the irises die.
That the cadmium bolt from the anther.
That the hollyhocks thrust forth impermanence
    I recognise, that my cat
finish in the bottlebrush, half closing her eyes
turned out upon shadow to recognise herself
in what the sun does, and the bees possessive barter
with the pistil, in ceremonial operations of dispersal
and return, reticulated footprints up the vine
    the surest sign of freehold.
That they have cause to sorrow, the bad water
the bald light pacing the growth of foxgloves. That the dark
    side of the sage leaf hide
the fragrance of the herb. To draw
    new colonies we grew felicia
daisies in a dozen places up the hillside
    but from the way the workers'
dance had changed, from trembling to swaying so
dispassionate the petals hardly tipped, I recognised
    the once good air
had weaponised, and how each breath I took
sold back to blossom but a fraction of the gust its greeny
    muscles manufactured
that the calyx self-propel her clutch
    of seed. That the rain
of atoms overhead erase the easy
    credit of the dead. That I choke

on smoke of sacrificial bergamot, its papal
   mauve, but weep not, keep
my salt aloft to spare this funeral earth.

YES OR NO

Are you happy
with your service

provider?

Have you contemplated
private

piety's
competitive prices?

Are you in the market
for something like

but not precisely
eternal return?

Have you been waiting long
in our baffled room?

Did you retain
a trace

of transmigration
somewhere like a scar

inside your
photographic

memoir?

Do you think birds feel
the seism?

Are you reading enough
of the novel

grovelling,
the genuine

genuphobia,
our nationwide

aversion
to kneeling?

Are you still listening

to poets
who listened

to Coltrane

laugh and framed
vocations around that

brazen ascesis?

Is there someone
in your family

we can call
to drive you home,

a flyover town

waiting around
for potable

blood to flow,
for prescription

prices to drop on
crushed-up rocks

from the moon?

Are you watching
not a little

terrified
as advertising

bromides
slowly embalm

the once
in a century mind

of your favourite
Thomist

on Twitter?

Can you hear
the siren

everything we ask you
feeds

flatter you now

beneath the waves
of what we need

to tell you?
Are you

sitting down?

MOUNT EDEN

Six pips
when the apparently real

grace relents
and the morning news begins

a mother's voice
pitchless in the day's chorale.

Grief so total
it resembles abundance

chastened
by the paradox of surplus

in a very bad year.
Exchanging

one indifferent signal
for another

you adjust
your figment's threshold

a pinnate leaf's width
on the dial

to find the season's violence
sensible again

repeated
in the weather whisperer's

impartial mysticism.
Such severe

report
like fanfare as you push

the leaves from yard to yard
all because

a little air has left the world.
The warnings turn

to traffic
and you to the sweeping under

blank façades
where later you will shake the olive

and the bay
and you will gather up

their bloodless panes
anything to stretch this needless

peace another hour.
The trees are not deciduous

enough.

KETTLE'S YARD

The kingdom will have its own colours,
and the unfashioned light will let itself be mastered
in a bottomless, Brancusi pool.
Metal refined by its own thinking force
retains that mercury peril,

       continues
to reflect the furious pleasure
of a man being listened to, the one who explains,
art become epiphenomenon of explanation,
a nuclear residue cheaper to tame,

        grace nostalgia
strident, even here

     where the Gaudier-Brzeska
holds the uncomfortable end of her posture,
sinews bright in the light nursery,
and light in the pits

     and mistakes.

AEVUM MEASURES

not of one bird but of many

abide more tritone idle mode
do not profane what God made clean

  in rhythms bald
    as winter trees
  in melodies
    of species lost
  to climate change
    forgotten words
  like Byzantines
    like holocenic
  wattlebirds
    are levitating
  emeralds
    in Peter's dream
  like seraphim
    and butterflies
  their wings have eyes

abide more tritone idle mode
and tell us something radical

   as cockles swim
     or scuttle
  for hollowed hull
    and drawing breath
  in darkness mull
    infallible
  and out of breath
    bewilder

abide more tritone idle mode
the dominant's a leaky still

  for quiet divination
    for every thought
  a finger on
    the fret-
  board's shifting centre
    where nothing dearer
  than the pure heart's
    purring minor
  requires demonstration

abide more tritone idle mode
the poor heart's pooling mirror

  for rivers must
    reverse upon contrition
  not by rote alone
    deliver
  trembling notes
    in honeyed throats
  the cardinals call
    the passerine tradition
  il stil novo
    as cockles cling
  to boats they know

abide more tritone idle mode
the shaper and the shaper's skill

   made sharpest corners
     spherical
   while desperate will
     sequestered crept
   in steady brass
     the skid to dread
   we cringe
     that man carves flesh
   out of himself
     a flying V
   the tympanum
     a temporary residence

abide more tritone idle mode
the rosy cross in domic hush

   the rosy wheel
     of perfect fifths
   the melodist
     with rigged guitar
   embellishes
     with mordents pricked
   from erstwhile soaring
     albatross
   what miracle
     so much of pain
   could make it past
     your theist brush
   your mark of Cain
     where airplanes rush
   and hostile trace
     abandoned ships
   in space

abide more tritone idle mode
despite the light your light deprives

  we see it crest
    in savage angel
  changefulness
    in *fauxbourdon*
  where devils scourged
    Gregorians
  in antiphon
    where any pleasure
  fifths afforded
    flights aborted measure
  notes neglected bird-
    inflected
  space a bird denies

abide more tritone idle mode
recall the pilot's discourse on

   angelical emissions
     behind the wash
  of carbon clouds
     impassive iron
  though light may be
     in principle
  allowed
     to throttle angels
  where they sleep
     just to hear the sound

abide more tritone idle mode
unto whose eyes do eyes return

  your influence?
    a lady asks
  as *Agnus dei*
    in agony descends
  a caustic paint
    the ceiling drips
  disrupting clips
    of sequence hymn
  in service of
    the synonym for saint
  the stammerer
    while causing it

abide more tritone idle mode
the perky bruise begins to bloom

   in buttermilk
     the flesh of bird-
   brained Janequin
     and Ockeghem
   Gesualdo's
     on the waterboard
   while Taverner
     and Tallis practise
   neck-verse
     by the gallows tree
   whose birds keep time
     almost eternity
   Miserere mei
     domine

abide more tritone idle mode
the inner ear's a misused dome

  a catacomb
    of counterfeited
martyr spines
    and huia spurs
that causes pain
    kilometres
above the ground
    where passengers
interpret what the trumpet
    and the cymbal mean
the pilot grabs
    his microphone
to tell the people
    what they heard

abide more tritone idle mode
the figured base the faithful strum

   as obstinate
    as rivers drum
   their delta mouth
    with sediment
   the sea espied
    at such removes
   its quality
    is personhood

abide more tritone idle mode
as breezes strip the trees' array

  and branchlets sieve
    the choicest light
  across the sourceless
    manuscript
  where nodding off
    the pilot cannot
  pry apart
    the words he reads
  from birds he's hearing die

abide more tritone idle mode
because of sin the artisan

cannot exact
　immaculate
the transept rose
　in damask steel
cannot restore
　with faithfulness
the hawthorn's scent
　to Amor's nose
it vanishes
　like God behind the opulence
and blows apart
　cannot impose his art
on better likenesses
　his compass froze
his eye is glass
　his clairaudition
rendered less
　each rose he sketched
in needless repetition
　whose lot is worse
that he alone survive
　interrogation
but cannot make them look
　alive

abide more tritone idle mode
if ear to ear these sins commit

   as shorebird sips
     her scallop
  a peregrine
     hears shorebird sup
  and stoops to her
     non-cochlear
  the only note
     she'd know him from
  diminished

abide more tritone idle mode
the stiff Guidonian finger

  he gave thee it
    to give the fig
  with fists in perfect
    impotence
  that we by rote
    divided both
  the sea the boat
    the hand the shell
  is braced within
    from *mi* to *fa*
  our thumbs withdraw
    to strings they are
  made dulcet by
    with dulcimer
  let them combine
    till memory
  commit this thing
    from C to C
  all-flattening

Guido C. had read 'Monologion'

THE NEOPLATONIST THEATRE

In the neoplatonist theatre
audience exists, a couple

of victims of the new
conscription, waiving

all their outrage,
waiting in the cockpit.

One's a former gallery
serf, feeding frozen

grapes to animals
not born to work

their mandibles that way.
One expresses gently

the gland whence prayers
discharge, a man

who sits and glares
at his companion, lost

in the foreignness
and novelty of names

his gland would praise
but can't forgive.

Some overeager, out-
of-tune apologist

announces tea
and biscuits in the vestibule.

Neither budge, rooted
in middlebrow certainty

that a single righteous
and timely volume

of samizdat applause, lodged
like a socket wrench

in the uptake, would stay
the launch of a still

more secretive
and stylised soliloquy.

BUBBLES

Lent, 2015

At home with contingency
breeze arrives like a first
principle. Autumn.

Red leaves welcomed, one
by one, into the yawning
corridor. A season's calm
demolitions, diminishing
returns,

imaginary saturations
of foliage on the threshold.

Window shocked
from the centre out, a spider
web ripple.

Transparency insurance,
daylight commandeering
other arms,

submarine lucidity.
A passage through
bathroom steam in a sequence

of traditions, the house
painter's wash-up
routine.

Nostalgia's exhausted
fanaticism, a little-
known need of the senses,

is enough to distress
the drywall

in memory. Thumbs squawk
across matte finish, fingernails set
against edification. Milk flesh
maturing

to olive by evening.

'The loudest quiet
street in Auckland.'

The crisis is dramatised
thus, this gently
noxious odour a neighbour's

responsibility. Privacy
delights in cautiously
collapsing distances.

The shower over an hour
ago, an aura
of warmth still clings to her.

Ropes of mist
enhance the typically
invisible line between
properties, slack there

so long a species of weed
might take hold

mid-air. Over the ambit
an argument in two
different languages,

mutually interpreted
with reference to a common
literature,

the myth of Narcissus.

Under the couches, into
the corners the dead leaves die

further. Zoning
precautions, inspectors.

Building an arbour
without any natives

is historical
windbreak, shade and the illusion

of seasonal change
for at least another decade.

Arrested development
whose ownership blurs
in real estate

legend. 'Twenty years
since construction began . . .

. . . there are Norfolk pines
younger

than the foundation.'

Her attention is an accident
of resistance, shattering
her reflection to get

clean, hammering
the water so hard she might be

forging an object
amid the speculation, fresh

masterpiece.

PIETRY

We deserve your boredom,
have wandered in and out of rage
like traders mapping an epic hedge.
This innocence award
more than compensates for what we've lost,
the peanuts of your patronage
that crumb the margins of a page
fortified against the Pentecost.

OAK PARK

Not wanting the quicker
figure walking

behind us to see us
suspicious, we project

curiosity in ailing brick.
The least architecture

confounds the cynic
arrhythmia: step, contra-step,

stop. The intervals
abridge themselves witless

the moment
a foreign body breaches

corporate shadow, exposing
a pinnacle, hidden

entrances, borders crossed
to be lived within

where the stucco invisibly
aspirates, and the citrus dim

pornography
flashes through a transom.

CHICAGO SKETCHES

Adventide, 2016

Commuter fragrance
on the wind's frontier

hurries potent
pheromones, designer fear

of the analogous
buzz, whatever -ism now

communism was
fifty-plus years ago.

Leaving the vigil
far-flung neighbours

commune around
the Rocket Popsicle

an ambulance makes
of a tavern half

smothered in drift.

Unmistakable
third-degree

thurible burns

on the homeless
teen's ankle.

Given the means
their mother would recast

the master bathroom
in travertine

and ebonised oak,
would blow

the western wall out,
more perfectly perform

the golden ratio
of what they earn

to what they owe.

Which rites of passage
roar tonight

from the hipster hotel?
A mitzvah? A marriage?

A non-commissioned
officer's ball.

An off-duty cop
nodding to sleep

in the handicapped spot.
A nervous father

gesturing apology
for his jumbo stroller.

A talkative sophomore
Forensics team

here to contend
having flown all the way

from Hackensack.
That's near New York

where no one hides
his garbage in the back.

One of two smokers
outside the Sovereign

approaches the other,
pretending to shiver.

'What's your brand?'

Misunderstanding,
he worries the cuff

of his Canada Goose.
Two horseshoe Omegas,

a fraternity scar.

The rarest Cardinals
cap, a carmine drip

on otherwise
untroubled snow.

JESUS GREEN

The kingdom will have its own spices
whose fore-scent is the privilege of a retriever
lifting her nose at last from the carcass.
When assorted corvids take her place
I will not whisper any of their names
to the tutelar of the college.

                The blue
roman candle advance of liberated students,
crossing the moat, appears from this distance
to embarrass the jogger,

                the avenue
of plane trees a parlour

                for homeless
who paddle through bugs like playing a harp,
plucking and smoking at once,
labour given lightness by caution.
I follow the sun down the darkening aisles
as if it were criminal.
The wind is animal with cannabis.

HYMN BEFORE A FEAST

Craft traps birds in grids
of pitch, each hash forbids
the feathered series flee.

Peer between crests
and watch the sand
retexture, as meshworks
drag the bottom flocks.

Fish too credulous
answer with a kiss
the jighead's dancer,
and the long rod dips
with their wounding.

Fields bequeath their native
treasure: ear-bearing
arms intense with lucre
and vine shoots nursing
festal fruits.

All this abundance,
sparing nothing, supplies
the slaves of Christ forever.

Inconceivable that hunger
whose satisfaction swells
the sanguineous channels
of factory farms.

Let pagans stuff
their young with slaughtered
breakfasts.

We await the green fur
of innocuous bean pods,
their diverse sorts.

We gurgle at the utter,
steep coagulant in milk,
and spread the tender
curdles into baskets.

We stoop beneath
the Attic combs and drain
the workers' dewy
tribute, their thyme-
inflected brews.

Wherever apple boughs
deliver, where thunder
earth with crimson bombs
we are.

Whose the trumpet?
Whose the fabulous guitar
could equal in timbre
the noise of our enjoyment?

STS. PETER AND PAUL

Auckland, 2014

An entire column scorched
from the daybook, so promise

no appointment, shirk
an afternoon jog. The listing

for Cancer was cryptic today,
almost cruel given context:

'Joy to you, Athens, we've won.'
Were the blood-

air barrier to crash of a sudden
anyone could drown

in the desert, Bilad al-Sham.
That a tiny adjustment of pressure

could render explosive a once
blameless thing, no sources confirm

exactly what pace
would have gotten that messenger

safely to Marathon.
Yesterday's wisdom said, 'Run

as one able to speak, un-
able to sing.'

A cold coming we had of it,
and the local children embarrassed

to see an adult at the font
who appeared to be drowning

an infant. Such was the light
at that hour, the season, the woods

parcelling sight out like a viridescent
jube, the trees replenished

for ordinary time. Embarrassed
and confounded to see an adult

in a summer suit startle
at the coolness of the water

and the unfamiliar scent
of the unguent: pomegranate,

palm, apple. And afterward
to misperceive the newly washed

as newly invested, pacing
under oak stands like a nursing

insomniac, pounding
the back of a colicky prince.

Confounded to enragement,
to watch this regicide

strolling free, without his lady
attendant, or helpmeet to follow

a clutchable distance behind
who proceeds from the Father

and Son. With the Father and Son
worshipped and glorified.

Misprision's mine,
a privilege. Perpetual

apprentice to reproof,
reminder. I only deny

what I cannot finish,
fictions hobbled by

their contests of miracle,
where every second

word's an accusation
and every third an alibi.

Domine, quo vadis?
I'm playing for time, I'm

wagering away whichever
foot might stumble me

first across the threshold
in reverse. I'm cutting

my loss. Hang me breech
if only to rehearse my birth.

To be like his glorified body
the content of a secret

exposure, the music
was arranged to be virtually

unperformable. The composer's
instructions require the total

conversion of the concert hall.
The private boxes, shuttered.

The gods remodelled utterly.
For not even the wealthiest

patrons shall witness
the orchestra in its entirety

but merely glimpse one soloist
per parable in *Matthew*,

one decade in a century
of choristers, each of whom

was asked to smuggle songbirds
past security. *Perfecte conscius*

perfectae generationis.
In a movement of maximal

affiliation, the audience
begin to grow restless, openly

arguing among themselves
whether an assembly this

immense, this impossibly
in time, is not for all

intents and purposes
a military exercise,

a resurrection drill.

There was a Birth, certainly,
and anamnesis begins

even before the umbilical
noose is cut, my rhythm

loose within my mother's
gown, eyes already

irritants, remembering forms
the horse-drawn hearse

recoiled from.
It could have been worse.

I could have surfaced
upside down.

anxieties are not rectitudes

ST. MARY THE LESS

The kingdom will have its own currency.
I cannot see any from the pew,
but I know the rivers of this country
sing with cancelled sterling.
Like silver under water
                              mercy
will flicker through the feeling
of the reader
                    infinitesimally warming the air
until all of our salvos begin with *forgive me.*
We pray today
                    in a national rope
for the brokenness of what we do
                                        here
in memory, pray
                    the discordances
of an amateur choir perform that brokenness better
than harmony, pray like the nonagenarians
                                                  cough
and infants bray
                    from the back
                              the *Angelus domini.*

PICKSTOCK IMPROVISATIONS

The one. The one
in many. The many
in one.

The many. A song
that there might be
a song.

Vae mihi, si non
thomistizavero.
I fear the verb

is intransitive.
Imagine its operation
intensely enough

it bubbles into law,

surfaces unfurrowed,
expressionless.

Woebegone,
begin again

by asking the wrong question:

Does the speed of sound
exceed
the quantity of the clarified?

The subtlest consolations
arrive in waves

one had neglected
to observe.

The way children
when they sing
forget to breathe.

Now-
now. There-
there.

They fix a distance
as if between strings

which beings bridge
for the pleasure
in their fingertips.

Needless dynamics
but *claritas* in one

salutary chord.

And in the time
between chords,

the means. No depths,
only lavender shallows.

One must choose modestly.
One note too many
and the nosegay
will tear your face away.

Astonisher.
Sophia, know that our clatter
is not disarmament.

To repeat identically

imagine the insanity

of the man who explains

who swears he sees

radio waves

boiling through the breeze.

The liturgy is aeviform
or boomerang of movements.
No moon of *Aufhebung*.
Only emanation then return.

The same differently
and always already:

after writing *laïcité*
new laity like birdsong.

LORIOT

the covert provenance
of each keyed motive

archives herself in loud
improvident plumage

our gamut's less raucous
more knowingly slowing

theology down
like a starved wind with

every concord conquered
even as its promised

calmness lizards into
other forms of human

perseverance
homophonous preserve

of fidelity
radically lived

IN MEMORIAM

.This marginal, windswept
allotment, withheld by fugitive

huge elms from full sun, obliges
what kind of care? Hinds

with eyes like almonds daily graze
the oat, and aphids dust

the cereals inedible. Weeks
of drought, and never rain without

the mission creep of dripping
members of invasive vines.

To ache over harvest, hark
but never hear the locusts come,

a nematode in either ear,
is too much struggle, a single

scabby currant for your trouble.
But if, even waist-deep

in effluent channels, in sunken
corners of a salted field, you build

your quarters, fix a pallet
from a heap of neutered cones,

there you might rest yourself
watchful, rapt enough to see

the new corn's tassel like a crucifix
pierce the vaulted manure.

AGNUS DEI

Must be a stumbler, bleeder,
as some floccus remains here, carded
into ragged sleeves by barbed wire.
I believe in a God who can learn

to work new spindles, new pupils
uncomprehending the reasons
light rosins in winter, and still
spill clumsily, bleeding.
Now drizzle caught

in oily pockets loads the fleece
with wealth. I've often wondered
what the fence keeps out
in a country bereft of predators.
I long ago reconciled

instinctive sympathy
for the perfect innocence of animals
with an equally ardent carnivory.
Arms retreat guilt-free

through the widest breach
in the garment, having chosen a meal
the stauncher faiths call impassible,
withdrawing to empty folds.
I hope you feel safe when you die.

THE POST-HORN

extempore raids
on sainthood no

recording twins
no audience

released upon
the blest without

a fruit to throw
the choice of Eden's

Jonathans
whose ripeness

never settles red
no caul

or nimbus rinds
that trepanned skull

lest we surmise
the innocence

they symbolise
and sloughing off

the scales withdraw
to gardens blamed

for empty quires
where sunflowers

heavy-haloed lean

DANTIS AMOR

Between salutation and salutation,
in that barely discernible *khôra*,
the landscape discovered
by neither watchman, she's astir.
A canon repeats for the final time
its memorial inventory—pomegranate,
palm, apple—all but irrecoverable
in *scordatura*, assaulting the follower
with unfamiliar bowing, despised
like sloshy mannerism, forgotten as swiftly
as Florentine deportment, as Kore Soteira,
as wafer dissolving in water.
To exist exhausts the host.
In private, I call her AMOR VENTURI.

THE NUPTIAL YES

. . . a riveder le stelle

Not to see but see AGAIN
 when I wasn't looking. See
AGAIN, when I was most
 benighted, and thus myself unseen.
Do I suggest, without intending,
 benign accompaniment?
Attention: my innumerable twin.
 Imagine two friends
with beautiful wings embracing.
 Imagine their embrace is a tree
without end. Without a flute
 of flower, the tree yet
fruited. Power is a fig thereon,
 the furthest droop. Imagine
one friend tastes a fig
 the other is forbidden.
The other does not eat, only
 watches with affection,
sees AGAIN fondly, though
 coercion is implied.
But at whose beck?
 Is the sequence leashed to its prime
articulation? *Sidus*
 absconditum. If the star
is hidden, that it wasn't sought
 annihilates the difference.

My lover says my gaze is
    fraught, is unintermittent,
is rarefied, is set ablaze.
    Our first encounter lingers
not a pattern but
    an emanation in the train
of every after. Its matter
    subtles. When like things ease
their spirit bubbles out a ways.
    I see AGAIN: the first inheres
in the second wing, creates
    the space in which eternals meet.
I see them touch their strings
    in thanks, see AGAIN
their contours interanimate.
    Voluptuous, the resultant
species, yes, but not itself
    the bass whereby all voices
balance. If the subjects meet
    before the finial seat is crossed,
the gaze is lost in the arbour
    of all others. When the star
of grace reticulates
    my lover, who, pray tell,
reciprocates? I see AGAIN
    but never direct. An arabesque
of mirrors intercedes.
    See AGAIN identity deepen
when alteration obtains

the furthestness of the fixed.
Coamantis. Imagine
  two friends, each other facing,
in mutual contemplation.
  It is considerable, their resolve,
the thousand upon thousand
  instruments involved
to see AGAIN the tension,
  forthspinning from within,
a doublecone. See AGAIN
  the concrete hierarchy
soften. See for the first what I
  had always known AGAIN
transmits a light it doesn't own.

NOTES

The dedication is taken from the first volume of Olivier Messiaen's *Traité de Rythme, de Couleur, et d'Ornithologie* (1949).

'Aevum Measures': *Aevum* denotes the measure of endurance enjoyed by the angels, the saints and other celestial creatures. In the *Summa Theologiae* (1265–1274), Thomas Aquinas defines *aevum* as the mean between mortal *time* and divine *eternity* (I.10.5). Like God, *aeviternal* beings have permanence of existence; their nature is subject neither to diminishment nor to change. However, with an unchangeable existence they have, like humans, 'changeability of choice'. The epigraph comes from Ezra Pound's 75th Canto.

The epigraph introducing the second section is taken from Ezra Pound's 105th Canto.

'Oak Park' is dedicated to Peter O'Leary.

'Hymn Before a Feast' adapts (it is *not* a translation) a segment of *Hymnus Ante Cibum* by the fourth-century Roman Christian poet Aurelius Prudentius Clemens.

'Sts. Peter and Paul': The liturgical feast in memory of the martyrdom of Sts. Peter and Paul, observed on the 29th of June, coincides with a number of historical events referenced more or less explicitly in the poem. Italicised lines quote T.S. Eliot's poem 'Journey of the Magi' (1927), the apocryphal *Acts of Peter*, and the text of Messiaen's *La Transfiguration de Notre Seigneur Jésus-Christ* (1969), which in turn quotes Thomas Aquinas on the Transfiguration in *Summa* III.45.4.

The epigraph introducing the third section is taken from Geoffrey Hill's poem 'Psalms of Assize' from *Canaan* (1996).

'Pickstock Improvisations' is dedicated to Catherine Pickstock and takes its primary inspiration from theological reflections contained in her books *After Writing: On the Liturgical Consummation of Philosophy* (1998); *Truth in Aquinas* (co-authored with John Milbank, 2001); and *Repetition and Identity* (2013). '*Vae mihi, si non thomistizavero*' ('Woe to me if I do not Thomisiticise') was a favourite saying of Jacques Maritain.

'Loriot': The Eurasian golden oriole (*Oriolus oriolus*), one of the birds whose song Messiaen transposed in his *Catalogue d'oiseaux* for solo piano, which was first performed in 1959 by the composer's wife and frequent collaborator, Yvonne Loriod.

'Agnus Dei' was inspired by Denise Levertov's poem of the same title from *Mass for the Day of St. Thomas Didymus* (1981). My love and thanks to Elaine Kahn for gifting me the final line.

'The Post-Horn' is dedicated to John Taggart. The title refers to a passage from Søren Kierkegaard's *Repetition* (1843):

> Long live the post-horn! It is my instrument, for many reasons, principally because one can never be certain of coaxing the same tone out of it twice. A post-horn is capable of producing an infinite number of tones, and the one who puts it to his lips and invests his wisdom in it will never be guilty of a repetition. (trans. M.G. Piety)

'Dantis Amor': The title of an 1860 painted panel by Dante Gabriel Rossetti, depicting Beatrice Portinari, beloved of Dante Alighieri. The panel, one of three cupboard doors of a large mahogany settle, first belonged to William Morris and is now housed in the Tate Britain. The coinage *Amor venturi* ('the love of what is to come') is taken from John D. Caputo's essay 'Spectral Hermeneutics' in *After the Death of God* (2007).

'The Nuptial Yes': The title comes from Simone Weil's essay 'The Love of God and Affliction' in *Waiting for God* (1950). The epigraph quotes the final words of Dante's *Inferno*.

ACKNOWLEDGEMENTS

I would like to express my immense gratitude to the editors and staff of the following publications where earlier versions of these poems appeared: *The Cultural Society*, *Fact-Simile*, *Verge*, *From a Compos't*, *The Spinoff*, *Dispatches from the Poetry Wars*, *Commonweal*, *Poetry*, *NZ Poetry Shelf*, *Sport*, and *The Winter Anthology*.

Many of the poems in *Lay Studies* were written with the generous support of a Victoria Scholarship, a residency at the University of Waikato, and a Grimshaw Sargeson Fellowship. My thanks to these bodies for their faith in my work. Thank you also to Creative New Zealand. Special thanks to the faculty, administrators, and students of the International Institute of Modern Letters.

Thank you, Fergus Barrowman, Ashleigh Young, Kirsten McDougall, Zach Barocas, Peter O'Leary, Chris Price, Norman Meehan, Damien Wilkins, Bill Manhire, Michele Leggott, Norman Finkelstein, Sarah Ross, Rowan Williams, Catherine Pickstock, Robin Kirkpatrick, John Taggart, Steven Manuel, Chris Holdaway, Jenna Todd, and Eleanor Catton.